Mealworms
Raise them, watch them, see them change

Written by Adrienne Mason

Illustrated by Angela Vaculik

Kids Can Press

Acknowledgment

Thanks to Robert Anderson, Research Scientist, Canadian Museum of Nature, Ottawa, Ontario, for his assistance in reviewing drafts of this book.

Text copyright © 1998 by Adrienne Mason
Illustrations copyright © 1998 by Angela Vaculik

Published in Canada by:
Kids Can Press Ltd.
29 Birch Avenue
Toronto, ON M4V 1E2

Published in the U.S. by:
Kids Can Press Ltd.
85 River Rock Drive, Suite 202
Buffalo, NY 14207

Edited by Valerie Wyatt
Designed by Marie Bartholomew
Printed in Hong Kong by Sheck Wah Tong Printing Press Limited

CM 98 0 9 8 7 6 5 4 3 2
CM PA 98 0 9 8 7 6 5 4 3 2 1

Canadian Cataloguing in Publication Data

Mason, Adrienne
     Mealworms : raise them, watch them, see them change

Includes index.
ISBN 1-55074-448-8 (bound)   ISBN 1-55074-506-9 (pbk.)

1. Beetles as pets – Juvenile literature. 2. Meal worms – Juvenile literature.
3. Beetles – Larvae – Juvenile literature. 4. Insects – Juvenile literature.
I. Vaculik, Angela. II. Title.

SF459.B43M38 1997   j638'.5769   C97-931289-2

Kids Can Press is a Nelvana company

Contents

Meet a mealworm

What does this girl have in her hand? It's a mealworm.
Most pet stores raise mealworms as food for lizards
and turtles. You can buy them for a few cents each and
raise them in your home or classroom. Mealworms
don't take up much space, they're not hard to care for,
and they're full of surprises. What surprises? Follow the
instructions for starting a mealworm farm on the next
page and see for yourself.

Mealworms are insects. So are butterflies, ants, mosquitoes, bees and thousands of other creatures. There are several million insects for every person on Earth.

5

Raise some mealworms

You can raise mealworms and watch them change as they grow. To see
all the surprising changes, you'll need to keep your mealworm farm going
for six to eight weeks.

You will need:

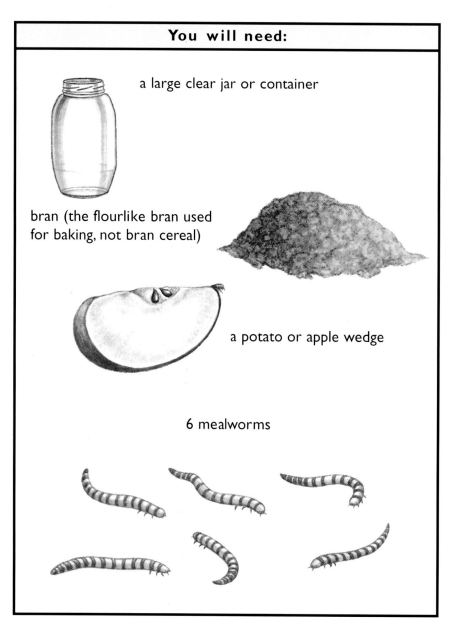

a large clear jar or container

bran (the flourlike bran used
for baking, not bran cereal)

a potato or apple wedge

6 mealworms

What to do:

1. Half-fill the jar with
bran. This will be the
mealworms' food.

6

2. Place the potato or apple wedge on the surface of the bran to provide moisture for the mealworms.

3. Add the mealworms and watch as they burrow into the bran.

4. Once a week, gently pour the contents of the jar onto a piece of paper. Over the weeks, can you find the four stages shown on pages 8 – 9?

5. Replace the potato or apple wedge if it becomes moldy or dried-up.

It's a fact

Mealworms, like all insects, do not have bones. Instead, they have a hard outer covering called an exoskeleton that protects and supports their soft body parts. As a mealworm grows, it sheds its too-small exoskeleton and grows a new one. Look for shed exoskeletons on the surface of the bran. A mealworm sheds its exoskeleton from nine to twenty times. The number depends on environmental conditions such as food supply and temperature.

What is happening to your mealworms?

Mealworms go through four stages – egg, larva, pupa and adult. The change from one stage to another is called metamorphosis, which means change of body form. Here is what happens at each stage.

1. Egg

A mealworm hatches from an egg smaller than the head of a pin. Because the egg is so small, it is very difficult to see it without a magnifier. Inside the egg, a small wormlike larva develops and grows. The larva hatches out of the egg in one to two weeks.

4. Beetle

The adult – called a darkling beetle – is soft and pale at first. Its skin darkens and hardens as it ages. The beetle lays up to 500 eggs and dies soon afterward. Then the cycle starts again – egg, larva, pupa, adult.

2. Larva

At first the larva may be difficult to
see because it is smaller than the exclamation mark
at the end of this sentence! But as it eats (and eats and
eats), the larva grows bigger and easier to see. It will molt
(shed its exoskeleton) and grow a new exoskeleton several
times. The larval stage lasts for an average of ten weeks.

3. Pupa

When it finishes growing, the larva changes into a pupa.
The pupa doesn't eat or move, but there are lots of things
happening inside it. The insect parts are rebuilt inside the
pupa, and the adult is formed. In two to three weeks, the skin
of the pupa splits open and the
adult beetle crawls out.

Metamorphosis

Most insects metamorphose. Why? By having two very different body forms, insects can share "jobs." For instance, the larva's job is to eat. The adult's job is to reproduce and to move around to find the best place for its babies to grow.

Some insects go through complete metamorphosis. Others go through incomplete (or simple) metamorphosis.

Complete metamorphosis

Complete metamorphosis has four stages – egg, larva, pupa and adult. Mealworms, as well as butterflies, bees, ants and flies, go through complete metamorphosis. Here is a butterfly metamorphosis. How does it compare with the mealworm metamorphosis on pages 8–9?

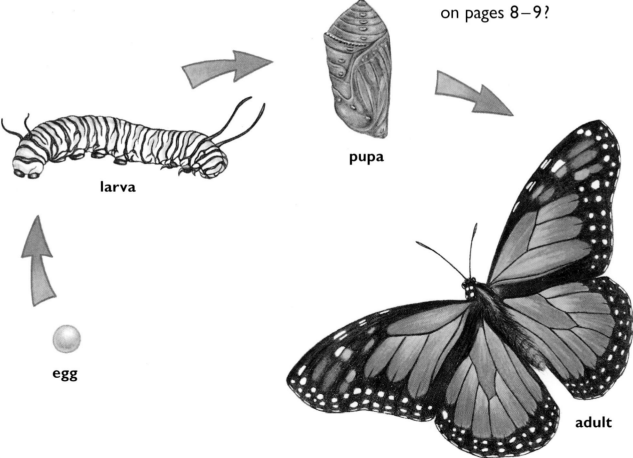

pupa

larva

egg

adult

Incomplete (or simple) metamorphosis

Some insects go through three stages, rather than four. This is called incomplete (or simple) metamorphosis. Here is the metamorphosis of a grasshopper. The grasshopper hatches from the egg looking a lot like a tiny version of the adult. This hatchling is called a nymph. When the nymph hatches, some of the adult parts, such as wings, are missing. As the nymph molts and grows larger, the adult parts slowly appear.

egg

nymph

adult

Metamorphosis match

Here are some familiar insects. Can you guess which type of metamorphosis these insects go through – complete or incomplete? Answers on page 23. Can you name each stage of metamorphosis for these insects?

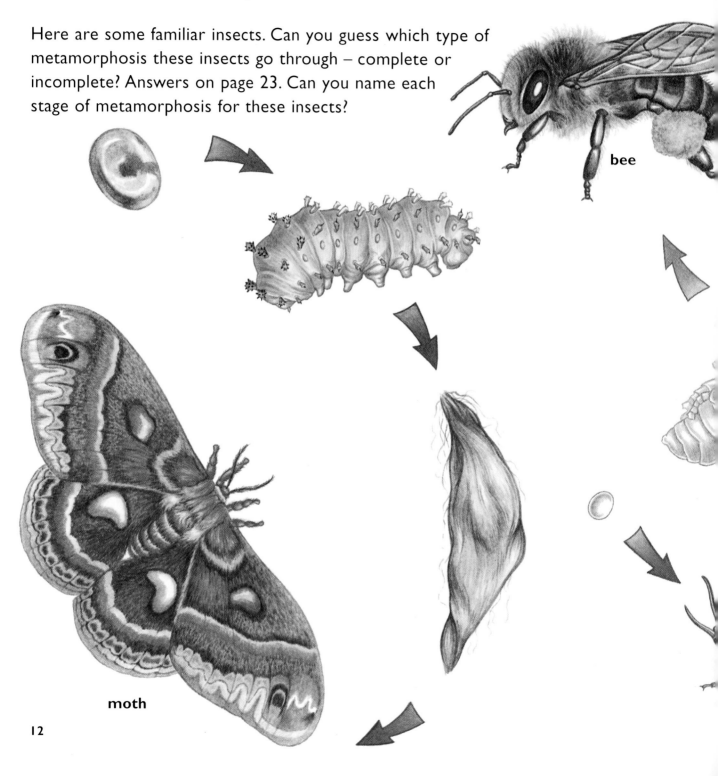

bee

moth

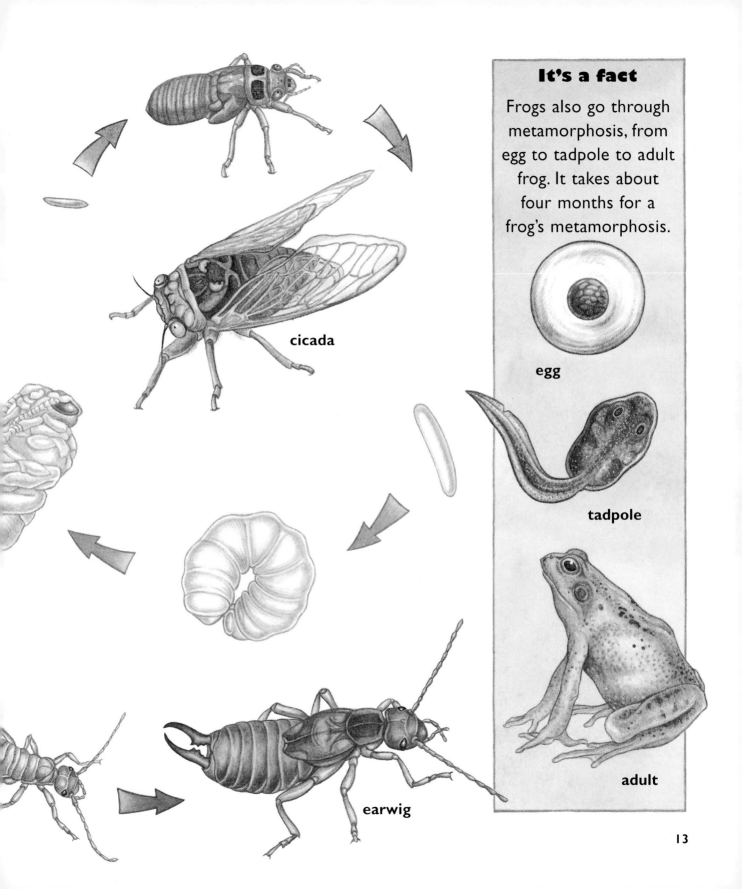

cicada

earwig

egg

tadpole

adult

13

Insect investigators

Mealworms are one type of insect. There are thousands of other kinds of insects. Some of them live in your backyard or neighborhood park. Make an insect catcher to see how many different kinds you can find. Also try to find insects at different life stages, such as those shown on pages 12–13.
Caution: Do not try to catch bees and wasps (they may sting) or insects with large delicate wings that are easily damaged.

What to do:
1. Cut the ends off the straws. Throw away the ends.

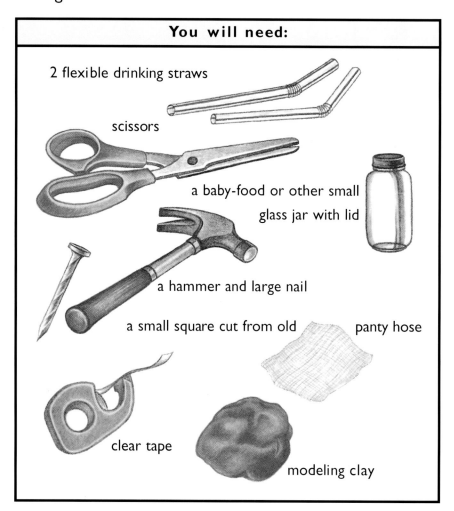

2 flexible drinking straws

scissors

a baby-food or other small glass jar with lid

a hammer and large nail

a small square cut from old   panty hose

clear tape

modeling clay

You will need:

2. Ask an adult to punch two holes in the jar lid using the hammer and nail. The holes should be big enough for the straws to fit into. Put one straw into each hole.

3. Use modeling clay to seal the spaces between the straws and the lid.

4. Tape the panty hose over the lower end of one straw.

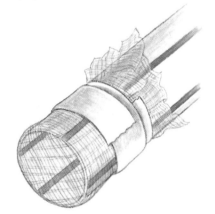

5. Screw the lid back on the jar.

6. Put the straw without the panty hose near the insect you wish to examine. Suck on the straw with the panty hose end. The insect will be sucked into the jar, where you can observe it. Compare the creatures you collect with your mealworms.

7. When you have finished looking at your insects, put them back where you found them.

Mealworms up close

Insects range from beetles smaller than the dot on this "i" to moths bigger than a dinner plate. Some insects fly, others swim or crawl, but all insects have:

- six legs
- three body parts (head, thorax and abdomen)
- two antennae

Take a closer look at the mealworm and darkling beetle on these two pages. If you have your own mealworms, use a magnifying glass to identify the body parts labeled below.

Mealworm (larva)

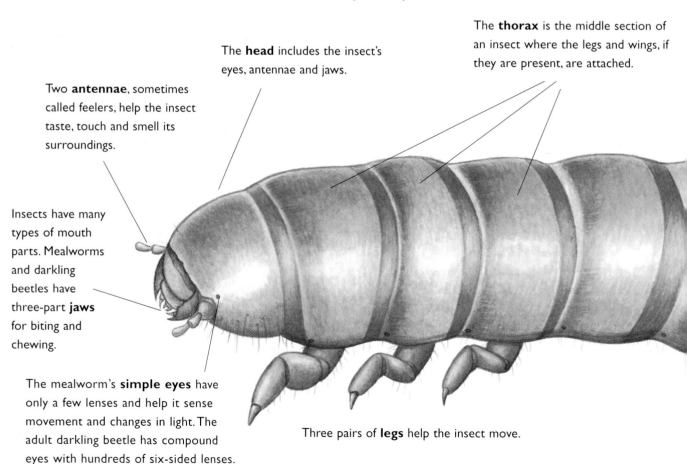

The **head** includes the insect's eyes, antennae and jaws.

The **thorax** is the middle section of an insect where the legs and wings, if they are present, are attached.

Two **antennae**, sometimes called feelers, help the insect taste, touch and smell its surroundings.

Insects have many types of mouth parts. Mealworms and darkling beetles have three-part **jaws** for biting and chewing.

The mealworm's **simple eyes** have only a few lenses and help it sense movement and changes in light. The adult darkling beetle has compound eyes with hundreds of six-sided lenses.

Three pairs of **legs** help the insect move.

Darkling beetle (adult)

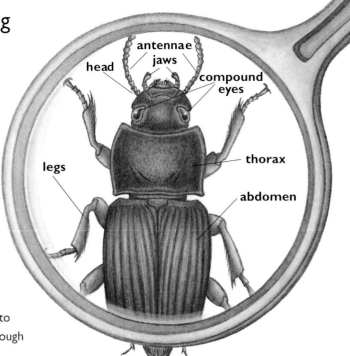

head — antennae — jaws — compound eyes — legs — thorax — abdomen

Instead of lungs, an insect uses a system of small tubes to carry oxygen through its body. Air enters the tubes through tiny holes called **spiracles** on the sides of the insect.

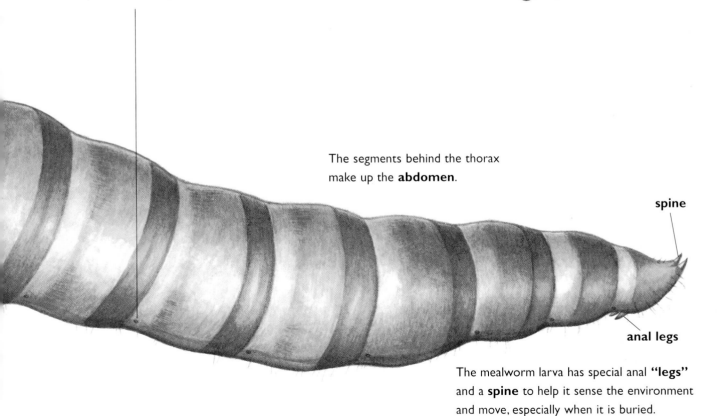

The segments behind the thorax make up the **abdomen**.

spine

anal legs

The mealworm larva has special anal **"legs"** and a **spine** to help it sense the environment and move, especially when it is buried.

17

Where do mealworms live?

Every living thing has a habitat, a place where it finds food, shelter, water and the space it needs to survive. A bowl of bran and some apple or potato wedges provide the habitat for your mealworms. But what about mealworms in the wild? What kind of habitat do they prefer? Here are some experiments to help you find out.

<table>
<tr><td align="center">You will need:</td></tr>
</table>

small mounds of bran, shredded leaves, toothpicks, grass and shredded wax paper

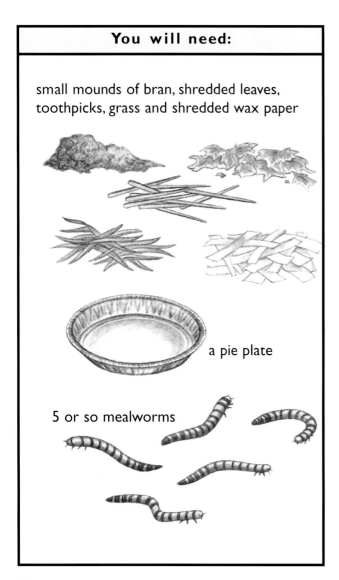

a pie plate

5 or so mealworms

Experiment 1:

Home sweet home

What to do:

1. Put the bran, leaves, toothpicks, grass and wax paper in separate piles around the edges of the pie plate.

2. Place the mealworms in the center of the pie plate. Watch the mealworms for ten minutes. Which "home" do they prefer?

Experiment 2: Wet or dry?

You will need:

2 sheets of paper towel

a pie plate

clear tape

5 or so mealworms

What to do:

1. Put one paper towel on half of the pie plate and tape down the edge as shown.

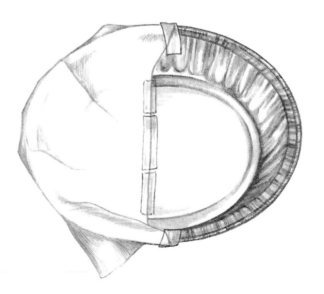

2. Lightly dampen the other paper towel and lay it over the other half of the pie plate.

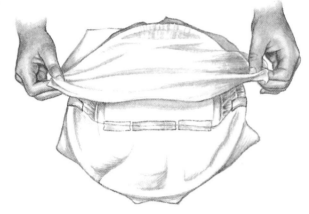

3. Put the mealworms in the center of the pie plate. Which side do they prefer? The wet or the dry?

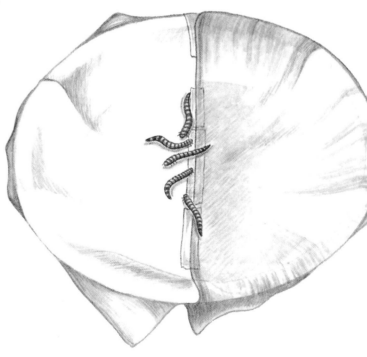

Experiment 3: Light or dark?

You will need:

a small box with a lid
(a shoe box works well)

scissors

5 or so mealworms

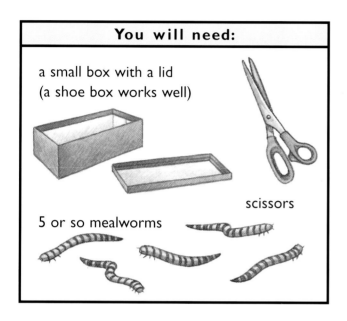

What to do:

1. Cut the lid in half. Put it on the box.

2. Place the mealworms in the middle of the box and observe. Which side do they prefer? The light or the dark?

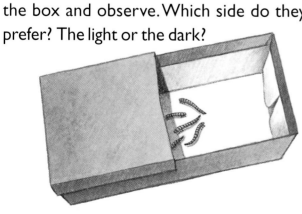

Now that you know what conditions mealworms prefer, which habitat do you think they would choose?

A swamp?

A desert?

A barn with stored grain?

What do mealworms eat?

Mealworms are usually found in grains stored in grain bins, barns, farms and kitchens. Give your mealworms a choice of food and see what they prefer.

You will need:

apple slices and a spoonful each of bran, cereal flakes (any kind) and peanut butter

a pie plate

5 or so mealworms

What to do:

1. Place the apple slices, bran, cereal flakes and peanut butter in separate mounds around the edge of the pie plate.

2. Put the mealworms in the center of the pie plate. Which foods do your mealworms prefer?

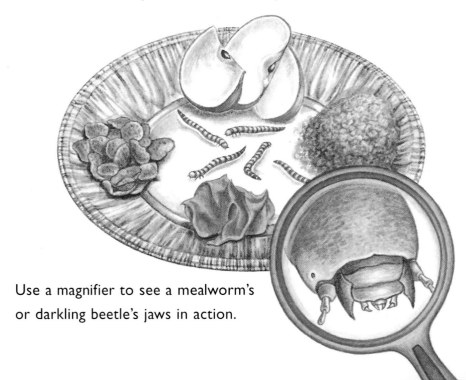

Use a magnifier to see a mealworm's or darkling beetle's jaws in action.

22

Glossary

adult: a fully grown animal that usually reproduces

exoskeleton: the hard outer covering that protects and supports an insect's body parts

habitat: a place where animals have the food, shelter, water and space they need for survival

insect: an animal that has six legs, three body parts (head, thorax and abdomen) and two antennae

larva: the stage of an insect or other animal that comes from an egg

life cycle: the stages of development (birth, growth, reproduction and death) that all living things go through

metamorphosis: a process that some animals undergo as they grow from egg to adult. It involves several changes to their body form.

molt: the process by which an insect sheds its exoskeleton as it grows

pupa: the stage in an insect's life cycle when the larva changes to an adult

reproduce: to create new life

Answers

Page 12: The moth and wasp undergo complete metamorphosis. The cicada and earwig undergo incomplete metamorphosis.

Index